Leckie
the education publisher
for Scotland

National 5
Biology
Lab Skills

for SQA assessment

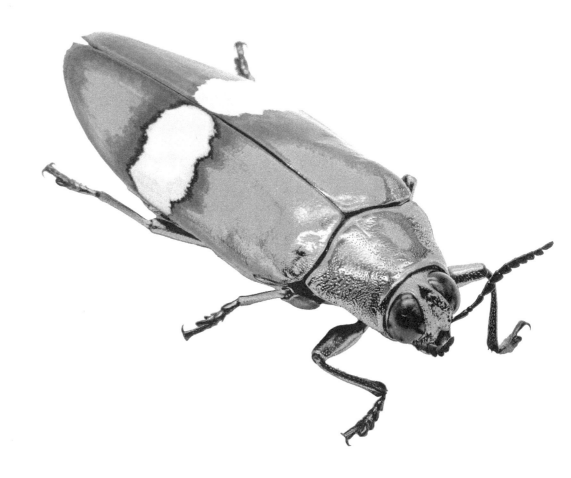

Billy Dickson & Graham Moffat

001/24012019

10 9 8 7 6 5 4

ISBN 9780008329631

Published by
Leckie
An imprint of HarperCollinsPublishers
Westerhill Road, Bishopbriggs, Glasgow, G64 2QT
T: 0844 576 8126 F: 0844 576 8131
leckiescotland@harpercollins.co.uk www.leckiescotland.co.uk

HarperCollinsPublishers
Macken House, 39/40 Mayor Street Upper, Dublin 1, D01 C9W8 Ireland

A CIP Catalogue record for this book is available from the British Library.

Publisher: Sarah Mitchell
Commissioning Editor: Gillian Bowman
Managing Editor: Craig Balfour

Special thanks to
Jouve India (layout, illustration and project managment)
Dr Jan Schubert (proofreading)
Jess White (copyediting)

Contents

How to use this book

Scientific skills are important for any science qualification. Your SQA National 5 Biology course develops the following skills and allows you to become familiar with the following techniques. These can be tested in your **examination**.

Skills

Planning; selecting; presenting; processing; concluding; predicting; evaluating.

Techniques

Measuring enzyme reactivity; using a respirometer; using a potometer; measuring abiotic factors; using a transect line; measuring the distribution of organisms; measuring the rate of photosynthesis.

For your **Assignment** you must carry out an experiment and collect data for use in your report. You could consider using one of the experiments in this book.

Remember you can refer back to this book when revising skills for examinations and other tests or when planning your Assignment!

Each of the 10 experiments has the following sections.

Background biology

These introductory statements cover the underlying biology which is needed to understand the context of the experiment and could help with any Assignment based on it.

Learning outcomes

This is a summary of the skills you will develop during each experiment.

Aim

A clear statement of the aim of the experiment is given. Any conclusion must be based on this aim.

Apparatus list

Your teacher will ensure that all the apparatus you need for the experiment can be found in the laboratory. You can use this list to check that you have everything you need to start your work. Items listed in **bold** are those you need to be aware of for your examination.

Certain solutions in the apparatus lists are marked with *, please see Appendix 3: Notes for teachers for how to make these solutions.

Safety notes

You should be aware of safety when carrying out an experiment. These notes will help you be aware of any safety issues! Your teacher will advise on safety information for each experiment, so pay attention.

Precautions

We've included some precautions which will help to make your experiment more accurate, valid and reliable.

Method

Always make sure you read every step of the method before you begin work. This will help you avoid mistakes and will give you an idea of what outcomes to look for as you complete each step.

Record your results

For each experiment there is a place to record the results of your work. Make sure you keep your data tables, graphs, answers and notes clear and neat.

Check your understanding and Exam-style questions

For each experiment, there are questions designed to check your understanding of the work you've just completed. There is also an exam-style question to help you prepare for exam questions based on experimental and scientific inquiry skills. Skills questions in your exam are worth about 30% of the overall mark.

Assignment support

Your Assignment is worth 20% of your grade for National 5 Biology. For your Assignment you will have to carry out an experiment and collect your own results data. You could consider using a technique from one of the experiments in this book. You will also need to find related data by research. Your teacher will be able to help you make decisions about Assignment topics and methods. Make sure your teacher is happy with what you decide to do.

The table below shows a checklist of sections in an Assignment report, with descriptions of how marks might be gained. There is a grid in **Appendix 4** which could be used to plan an Assignment based on this checklist.

Section	Description	Marks
Title	The report has an informative title.	1
Aim	A description of the purpose of your investigation.	1
Underlying biology	A description of the biology relevant to your aim, which shows your understanding. You need a **minimum of three biology points** along with their descriptions or explanations at National 5 level. You must use your own words as much as possible.	3
Data collection and handling	A **brief** description of your experimental/fieldwork method. You must show that you can **summarise** your experimental/fieldwork method and **must not** give a full description.	1
	Sufficient data from your experiment/fieldwork.	1
	Data from your experiment/fieldwork presented in a table with headings and units.	1
	Values correctly calculated from your experimental/fieldwork data.	1
	Data/information from an internet/literature source that you can compare with the data from your experiment/fieldwork.	1
	A reference for the internet/literature source.	1
Graphical presentation	Appropriate type of graph used to present your experimental/fieldwork data.	1
	Suitable scales.	1
	Suitable labels and units on axes.	1
	All data plotted accurately. Have points which are joined with a line (line graph) or clear bar tops (bar chart).	1

Section	Description	Marks
Analysis	Experimental/fieldwork data compared to data/information from internet/literature source.	1
Conclusion	A conclusion relating to your aim, based on data/information in your report.	1
Evaluation	Identification of a factor affecting the reliability, accuracy or precision of your experiment/fieldwork **and** a related explanation. You must then explain either: • what you did or could have done to minimise the effect of this factor; or • how you know this factor had a significant effect.	2
Structure	A report which can be easily followed.	1
Total		**20**

1 Estimating plant cell size – Calculating the average length of an onion epidermal cell

Background biology

Plant cells have cell walls, which helps make them easily visible using simple microscopes. Coloured stains can be used to improve the visibility of plant cell structures even more. The epidermal tissue from onion is a great source of thin layers of plant cells.

Cell measurements are usually given in micrometres (μm). There are 1000 micrometres (μm) in a millimetre (mm) and 1000 millimetres (mm) in a metre (m).

Learning outcomes

- Know and understand that plant cells have a cell wall visible by microscope.
- Process information by converting measurements between millimetres and micrometres.
- Process information by calculating averages.
- Process information by calculating ratios.
- Present information as a line drawing.

Aim

To determine the average cell length in onion epidermis.

Apparatus list

- **dropper** and bottle of iodine solution* (1)
- glass microscope slide (1)
- cover slip (1)
- forceps or mounted needle (1)
- thin sample of fresh onion epidermis cut for you (1)
- light **microscope** (1)
- paper towel (1)
- paper tissue (supply)
- safety glasses (pair each)

Safety notes

- Iodine is harmful to the skin and eyes – use carefully and wear eye protection. Wash any spills with plenty of water.

Experimental precautions

- Try to have your onion epidermis flat against the slide – folds make observation more difficult.
- Try to lower the cover slip carefully to avoid air bubbles – forceps or a mounted needle should help.

Method

1. Set up your microscope according to your teacher's instructions.
2. Adjust the magnification to low power – ×40.
3. Have the objective lens as far from the stage as possible.

4. Place a clear plastic ruler onto the stage and focus on the scale.

5. Increase the magnification to ×100 and estimate the diameter of the field of view in millimetres using the ruler. Multiply your answer by 1000 to convert your estimate into micrometres. Record your result in the section below.

6. Place your microscope slide onto a paper towel and add a drop of iodine onto the middle of the slide.

7. Use forceps to add a small piece of onion epidermis to the stain and try to flatten it out.

8. Use the forceps to gently lower a cover slip.

9. Use a tissue to soak up any excess stain.

10. Observe your slide at ×100.

11. Swivel the slide on the stage so that the cells are lined up across the field of view, as shown in the diagram in the exam-style question on page 3.

Record your results

1. Add the field of view details to the boxes below.

2. Draw some of the cells you can see in the field of view.

3. Count the number of cells which can be seen across the diameter of the field of view.

4. Calculate the average width of one cell in the spaces below.

Figure 1.1

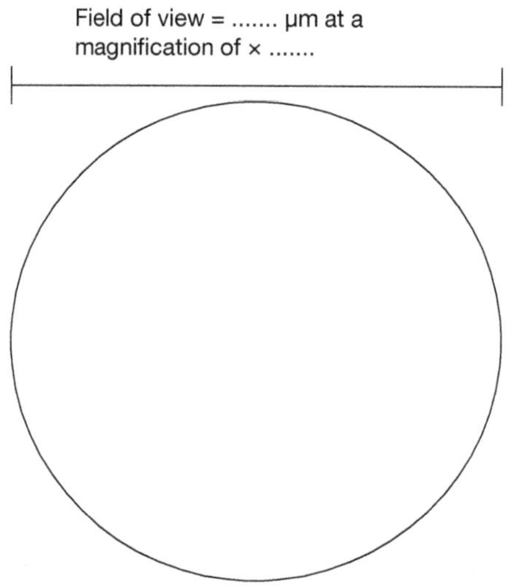

Field of view = ... µm at a
magnification of × ....

$$\frac{\text{Diameter of the field of view at} \times 100}{\text{Number of cells across the field of view at} \times 100} = \boxed{} \\ = \boxed{}$$

Average width of one onion cell = ... micrometres

Check your understanding

1. Explain why it's important to make a flat preparation of onion epidermis. [1]

   ....

2. Explain why it's useful to stain onion epidermis before viewing under a microscope. [1]

   ....

3. Express the following sizes in micrometres. [3]

   a. 5 mm   = ... µm

   b. 0·5 mm   = ... µm

   c. 0·05 mm = ... µm

Exam-style question

a. The diagram below shows the field of view of a microscope with some stained onion epidermal cells.

Field of view = 1·2 mm at ×100 magnification = 12 µm

Figure 1.2

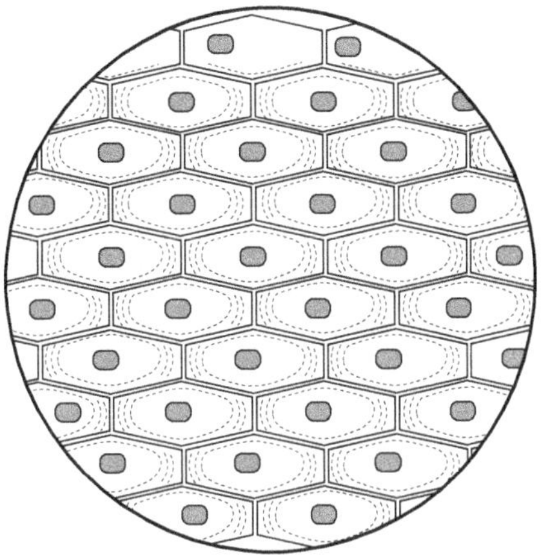

   i. Calculate the average estimated length and height in µm of one onion epidermal cell. [2]

   Length: .... µm

   Height: .... µm

   ii. Calculate the ratio of average cell length to average cell height in this example. [1]

   .... length : .... height

b. The diameter of a human red blood cell was estimated at 0·008 millimetres.

   Convert this value from millimetres into micrometres.

   .... µm [1]

c. Describe how a student could estimate the diameter of a human cheek cell. [4]

   ....

   ....

   ....

   ....

Assignment support

You could use this technique to generate data for your Assignment.

You could investigate whether the size of an onion epidermal cell depends on the variety, size or age of the onion. The oldest epidermal cells of an onion are in the outermost layers of epidermis.

You could use a copy of the grid in **Appendix 4** to plan an Assignment based on this technique – use the checklist on pages v–vi to help.

2 Osmosis – Measuring the effect of different water concentrations on the mass of potato tissue

Background biology

Water moves into and out of cells by osmosis. This process is passive so does not require an input of energy for it to occur. The water moves down the water concentration gradient from higher water concentration to lower water concentration, passing through the pores in the selectively permeable cell membrane and either into or out of the cells. In plant cells, movement of water inwards causes cells to swell with water and become turgid. Movement of water out of cells causes their vacuoles to shrink and the cells to become plasmolysed. Turgid cells increase in mass because of the water they contain. When left in a solution of equal concentration to the cell sap, no net movement of water occurs and there is no change in mass of the tissue.

Learning outcomes

- Know and understand the terms osmosis, turgid and plasmolysed.
- Control the variables in an experiment.
- Comment on the reliability of an experiment.
- Draw valid conclusions.
- Process information by calculating percentages.
- Present information as a line graph.
- Evaluate experimental procedures and suggest improvements.

Aim

To measure the effects of solutions of different water concentration on the mass of potato tissue

Apparatus list

- plastic **syringe** (5×10 cm^3)
- glass **beaker** (5×100 cm^3)
- cork borer (1 cm diameter)
- potato, peeled (5×2 cm cylinders)
- distilled water (100 cm^3)
- 1% salt solution (100 cm^3)
- 5% salt solution (100 cm^3)
- 10% salt solution (100 cm^3)

- 15% salt solution (100 cm^3)
- sticky labels (5)
- craft knife and tile (1)
- **timer** (1)
- two-figure digital **balance** (1)
- safety glasses (pair each)
- paper towels (supply)
- ruler (1)

Safety notes

- Cork borers and craft knives are very sharp – use them carefully, carry them with the cork cover on the blade and always cut downwards onto the tile.

Experimental precautions

- Be careful to make sure the potato tissue cylinders are the same length.
- Be sure to blot the surface of the cylinders with paper towels before weighing them.

Method

1. Set up five beakers and label them for the different solutions.

2. Add 30 cm³ of the solution to its labelled beaker using a different syringe for each.

3. Prepare five cylinders of potato tissue using the cork borer and craft knife. (Your teacher may have prepared these for you.)

4. Blot the surface of each cylinder with a paper towel and weigh each separately. Record the initial mass in the table below. Slide one potato cylinder into each of the beakers.

5. Start the timer and, keeping the beakers at the same temperature, time for as long as possible but for at least 20 minutes.

6. After a minimum of 20 minutes, remove each cylinder, blot it and reweigh it. Record the new masses in the table below.

Record your results

1. Calculate the percentage change in mass of each cylinder using the following formula and complete the table below.

$$\frac{\text{Final mass}}{\text{Initial mass}} \times 100\%$$

2. Plot the percentage change in mass against concentration of salt solution on the graph paper on the next page.

   Any gains in mass should be plotted above 0% on the graph and any losses in mass should be plotted below 0%. The graph line crosses the concentration axis at a concentration which gives no gain or loss in mass, and so that must be the concentration of the cell sap.

   Your teacher will help you with this.

Table of results

Salt concentration (%)	Initial mass (g)	Final mass (g)	Percentage change in mass (%)
0 (distilled water)			
5			
10			
15			
20			

Line graph of results

Figure 2.1

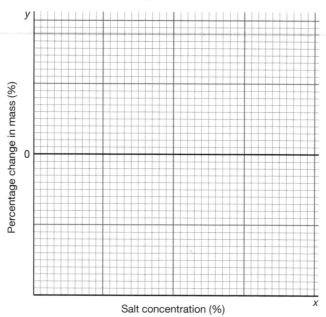

Salt concentration (%)

Check your understanding

1. Write a conclusion based on the aim of your experiment. [1]

    ....

    ....

2. Make a list of **three** variables which were controlled in your experiment. [3]

    1. ....

    2. ....

    3. ....

3. Suggest how the results of the experiment could be made more reliable. [1]

    ....

    ....

Exam-style question

In an experiment, the effect of salt concentration on potato tissue was investigated. The results are shown in the table below.

Salt concentration (%)	Initial mass (g)	Final mass (g)	Change in mass (g)	Percentage change in mass (%)
0	2·20	2·53	+0·33	+15
5	2·00	2·20	+0·20	+10
10	2·00	1.90	−0·10	−5
15	2·10	1·89		
20	2·10	1·40	−0·7	−30

a. Calculate the change in mass and percentage change in mass for the potato in the 15% salt solution and add your answers to the table above. [2]

b. Explain why percentage change in mass is a more valid way to express the results than the change in mass alone. [1]

....

....

c. It was suggested that the potato cell sap was equivalent to between 5 and 10% salt solution.

Explain how this can be justified from the results in the table. [2]

....

....

....

Assignment support

You could use this technique to generate data for your Assignment.

You could investigate many aspects of osmosis, such as investigating the effects of the concentrations of different solutes such as glucose or sucrose on potato or other plant tissue.

You could use a copy of the grid in **Appendix 4** to plan an Assignment based on this technique – use the checklist on pages v–vi to help.

3 Measuring enzyme activity 1 – Comparing catalase activity in different tissues

Background biology

Enzymes work as biological catalysts and are made by all living cells. They speed up chemical reactions in cells. Each enzyme is most active in its optimum conditions. Catalase is a common enzyme found in almost all living tissues. This enzyme breaks down the substrate hydrogen peroxide into the products water and oxygen in a degradation reaction. The activity of the enzyme can be studied by measuring the volume of oxygen produced when a sample of living tissue is placed into a container with hydrogen peroxide.

Learning outcomes

- Know and understand the terms enzyme, substrate and product.
- Control the variables in an experiment.
- Comment on the reliability of an experiment.
- Draw valid conclusions.
- Process information by calculating averages.
- Present information as a bar chart and as a line graph.
- Evaluate experimental procedures and suggest improvements.

Aim

To determine whether the rate of catalase activity is different in one type of tissue compared with another.

Apparatus list

- plastic **syringe** (1×2 cm^3)
- cork borer (1 cm diameter)
- **measuring cylinder** (4×10 cm^3)
- hydrogen peroxide (10 cm^3 of 3% solution)
- potato, sweet potato, carrot, turnip (1 disc of each)
- sticky labels (4)
- craft knife and tile (1)
- **timer** (1)
- safety glasses (pair each)
- ruler (1)

Safety notes

- Hydrogen peroxide is corrosive and can burn the skin and eyes – use carefully and wear eye protection and plastic gloves. Wash any spills with plenty of water.
- Cork borers and craft knives are very sharp – use them carefully, carry them with the cork cover on the blade and always cut downwards onto the tile.

Experimental precautions

- Make the tissue slices the same thickness so that they can be compared more easily.
- Work together with your partner(s) to ensure that step 4 of the method is done at one time.

8

Method

1. Set up four measuring cylinders and label each with the name of one of the tissues available.

2. Add 2 cm³ of 3% hydrogen peroxide to each using the plastic syringe. Take care!

3. Prepare a slice of each tissue using the cork borer and craft knife. (Your teacher may have prepared these for you.)

4. Slide each disc of tissue into its labelled measuring cylinder and start the timer.

5. Time the reaction for 30 seconds. During that time you should see bubbles of oxygen foam rising up the measuring cylinder scale.

Record your results

1. Record the volumes produced for each tissue and add your results to the table below.

   Remember that there is 2 cm³ of liquid and a slice of tissue already in the cylinder so, if you read the top of the foam, remember to subtract the liquid level value from the reading.

Figure 3.1

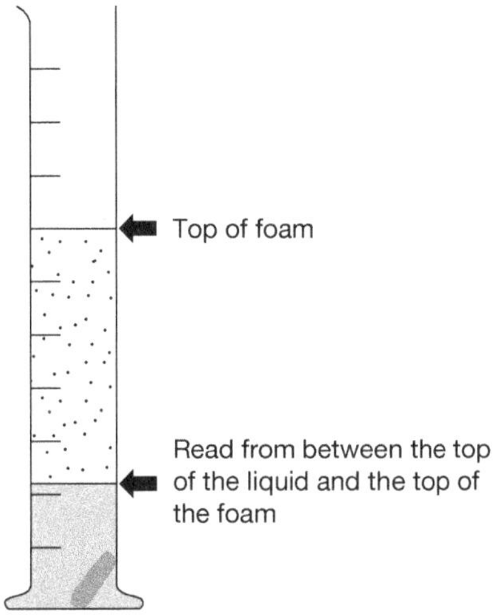

← Top of foam

← Read from between the top of the liquid and the top of the foam

2. Collect results from three other groups in the class and calculate an average volume for each tissue. Add the results to the table below.

3. Use the graph paper on the next page to draw a bar chart to show the average results for the class.

   Remember to add labels and units to your graph scales.

Table of results

Plant tissue	Oxygen foam produced (cm³)				Average volume of oxygen foam (cm³)
	Trial 1	Trial 2	Trial 3	Trial 4	
Potato					
Sweet potato					
Carrot					
Turnip					

Bar chart of results

Figure 3.2

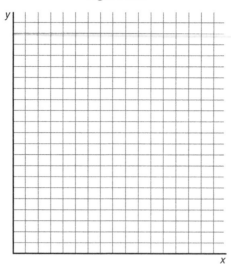

Check your understanding

1. Write a conclusion based on the aim of your experiment. [1]

    ....

    ....

2. Make a list of **three** variables which were controlled in your experiment. [3]

    1. ....

    2. ....

    3. ....

3. Evaluate your experimental procedure by identifying a potential flaw in the method and
    suggesting how that flaw could be overcome. [2]

    ....

    ....

    ....

    ....

Exam-style question

In an experiment, the effect of temperature on the rate of catalase activity was investigated. Potato tissue weighing 10 g was placed into each of six measuring cylinders containing 2 cm^3 of hydrogen peroxide and each cylinder was kept for 1 minute at a different temperature. The volume of oxygen foam was measured in each cylinder and the results are shown in the table below.

Temperature (°C)	Average volume of oxygen foam (cm³)
0	0·1
10	0·5
20	1·0
30	1·5
40	2·0
50	0·5

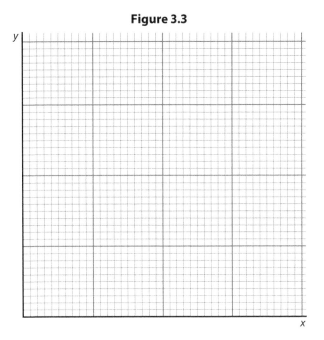

Figure 3.3

a. On the graph paper above, draw a line graph of the results. [2]

b. Describe the trend shown by the results in your graph. [2]

....

....

....

c. Describe how the procedure could be modified to test the effect of pH on the activity of catalase. [2]

....

....

....

Assignment support

You could use this technique to generate data for your Assignment.

You could investigate many aspects of enzyme activity, such as the effects of temperature, pH and substrate or enzyme concentration on catalase activity.

You could use a copy of the grid in **Appendix 4** to plan an Assignment based on this technique – use the checklist on pages v–vi to help.

4 Measuring enzyme activity 2 – Effect of temperature on the activity of diastase

Background biology

Enzymes work as biological catalysts and are made by all living cells. They speed up chemical reactions in cells. Each enzyme has an optimum temperature at which it is most active. Enzymes are proteins so they can be denatured by high temperature which changes the shape of their active sites. Diastase is an enzyme found in plants. This enzyme breaks down the substrate starch into the product maltose – a simple sugar in a degradation reaction. The activity of the enzyme can be studied by measuring starch breakdown in agar gel over a set period of time. When the gel is flooded with iodine, the area in which the starch has broken down will remain yellowish and not turn blue-black.

Learning outcomes

- Know and understand the terms enzyme, substrate and product.
- Control the variables in an experiment.
- Comment on the reliability of an experiment.
- Draw valid conclusions.
- Make a prediction.
- Present information as a line graph.
- Evaluate experimental procedures and suggest improvements.

Aim

To determine the effect of temperature on diastase activity in barley grains.

Apparatus list

- **dropper** and bottle of iodine solution* (1)
- **Petri dishes** with starch agar* (4)
- barley grains (soaked, washed in bleach, rinsed and cut in half) (10)
- sticky labels (4)
- forceps (1 pair)
- fridge (compartment set at 4°C)
- incubator or **water bath** (2, one set at 40°C and one set at 60°C)
- sticky tape (roll)
- safety glasses (pair each)

Safety notes

- Iodine is harmful to the skin and eyes – use carefully and wear eye protection. Wash any spills with plenty of water.
- Handle barley grains with forceps – they have been washed in a bleach solution!

Experimental precautions

- Place the cut surfaces of the grains onto the starch agar. Gently push down so the grain is just under the surface of the agar.
- Only open the Petri dishes to add the half grains and do that quickly.

Method

1. Label the underside of four Petri dishes with starch agar at 4, 20, 40 and 60°C.
2. Use forceps to add four half barley grains to each dish. Ensure that the cut sides are pushed into the agar and that the halves are well spaced. Take care!
3. Tape each dish with a couple of squares of sticky tape.
4. Place one dish in the fridge, leave one on a side bench, place one in the 40°C incubator and one in the 60°C incubator.
5. Leave the dishes for the same length of time – this must be for at least 24 hours.
6. Open each dish, flood the agar with iodine solution and leave for 10 minutes. Areas around the barley grains in which starch has been broken down will **not** turn blue-black.
7. Tip the iodine out of the dishes into the waste container provided. Try to avoid drips.

Record your results

1. Turn each dish over and use a ruler to measure the biggest diameter of any clear yellowish areas around the barley grains. Add your results to the table below.

    Remember that the clear yellowish area is a measure of the breakdown of starch – the larger the clear area the more starch has been broken down.

Figure 4.1

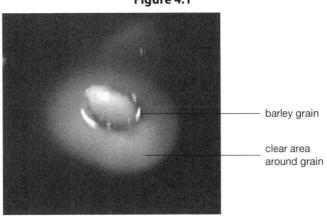

barley grain

clear area
around grain

2. Calculate the average diameter of the clear zone for each temperature. Add the results to the table below.
3. Use the graph paper on the next page to draw a line graph to show the average results.

    Remember to add labels and units to your graph scales – use the table headers below to help with this.

Table of results

Temperature (°C)	Measure of diastase activity				
	Diameter of clear yellowish area around each of the four grains (mm)				Average diameter of clear area (mm)
	1	2	3	4	
4					
20					
40					
60					

Line graph of results

Figure 4.2

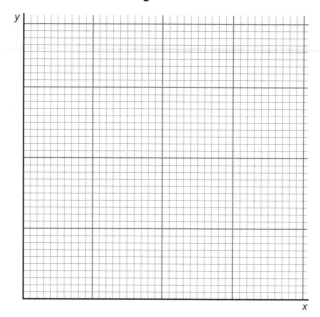

Check your understanding

1. Write a conclusion based on the aim of your experiment. [1]

    ....

    ....

2. Make a list of **three** variables which were controlled in your experiment. [3]

    1. ....

    2. ....

    3. ....

3. Evaluate your experimental procedure by identifying a source of error in the method and suggesting how that source of error could be corrected. [2]

    ....

    ....

    ....

Exam-style question

In an experiment, the effect of pH on the rate of diastase activity was investigated.

pH	Diastase activity (average diameter of clear area (mm))
5	2·5
6	4·0
7	6·5
8	4·0
9	2·0
10	1·5

a. On the graph paper below, draw a line graph of the results shown in the table. [2]

Figure 4.3

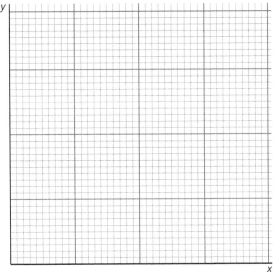

b. Write a conclusion to describe the effect of pH on the activity of diastase. [2]

....

....

....

c. Use the results to predict the diameter of the clear area which would be produced if the experiment were repeated at pH 8.5. [1]

....

....

....

Assignment support

You could use this technique to generate data for your Assignment.

You could investigate many aspects of diastase activity, such as the effects of temperature, pH and substrate concentration.

You could use a copy of the grid in **Appendix 4** to plan an Assignment based on this technique – use the checklist on pages v–vi to help.

5 Using a respirometer – Measuring the effect of temperature on the rate of respiration in germinating pea seeds

Background biology

Chemical energy stored in glucose is released by cells through a series of enzyme-controlled reactions called respiration. The energy is released is transferred by ATP to be used for cellular activities such as cell division and protein synthesis. The cells in germinating seeds respire aerobically, consuming oxygen from their environment. The volume of oxygen they take up can be measured in a closed container called a respirometer. Although the seeds also produce carbon dioxide gas in the process, this can be absorbed into a solid material such as soda lime so that the overall change in the respirometer gas volume is due to oxygen uptake only.

Learning outcomes

- Know and understand that respiring tissue takes up oxygen from its container.
- Process information by calculating averages.
- Present information as a line graph.
- Draw conclusions from results.
- Evaluate experimental procedures and suggest improvements.

Aim

To investigate the effect of temperature on respiration in germinating peas.

Apparatus list

- respirometer **boiling tube** with platform, bung and delivery arm (4)
- germinating pea seeds (supply)
- food-colouring liquid (supply)
- small bottle (4)
- ice bath (1 at 0°C)
- soda lime (supply)
- **water bath** (1 at 30°C)
- **timer** (1)
- ruler (1)
- **thermometer** (3)
- marker pen (1)
- safety glasses (pair each)

Safety notes

- Soda lime is harmful to the skin and eyes – do not remove it from the respirometer.

Experimental precautions

- Ensure the respirometer bungs are fitted tightly.

Method

1. Place three germinating peas onto the platform of each respirometer.
2. Add 5 cm³ of food colouring to each small bottle.

3. Fit each bung to each respirometer tube then place one respirometer in the ice bath, one on the bench and the other in the water bath and leave for 10 minutes.

4. Dip the end of each respirometer arm into the food colouring as shown in the diagram. **Mark the level of the liquid with a marker**.

Figure 5.1

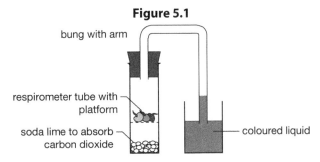

bung with arm

respirometer tube with platform

soda lime to absorb carbon dioxide

coloured liquid

5. Leave the sealed respirometers in their temperature for as long as possible but for at least 15 minutes.

6. Measure how far up the tube the coloured liquid rose in each respirometer.

Record your results

1. Add your results to the table below – make sure you measure the temperature of the room.

Temperature (°C)	Oxygen used (distance up tube (mm))	Average oxygen used (mm)
0		
Add the room temperature value here:		
35		

2. Collect results round the class and calculate the average oxygen consumption by the peas.

3. Plot a line graph of the class average results on the graph paper below.

Figure 5.2

y

x

Check your understanding

1. Write a conclusion based on the aim of your experiment. [1]

    ....

    ....

2. Make a list of **three** variables which were controlled in your experiment. [3]

    1. ....

    2. ....

    3. ....

3. Evaluate your experimental procedure by identifying a source of error in the method
    and suggesting how that source of error could be corrected. [2]

    ....

    ....

    ....

    ....

Exam-style question

A student investigated the effect of temperature on the rate of respiration in germinating (growing) peas.
Four respirometers labelled A–D were set up at the temperatures shown in the table below.

Figure 5.3

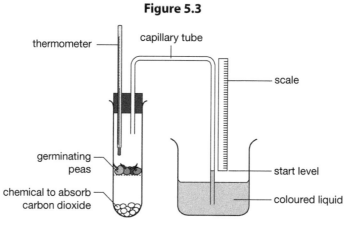

The level of the coloured liquid was measured on the scale at the start of the investigation and again after
20 minutes. The rise in liquid level was due to oxygen uptake by the germinating peas. The results are
shown in the table.

Respirometer and its contents	Temperature (°C)	Rise in level of liquid (mm)	Rate of oxygen consumption by the peas (mm per minute)
A Respiring peas	15	14	0·7
B Dead peas	15	0	0·0
C Respiring peas	25	26	
D Dead peas	25	0	0·0

a. Complete the table on the previous page by calculating the rate of oxygen uptake per minute by the peas in respirometer C. [1]

b. Write a conclusion which can be drawn from the experiment. [1]

....

....

c. Another respirometer was set up with germinating peas at 60°C and the coloured liquid did not rise. The student concluded that the peas were not respiring.

Suggest why this temperature prevented the peas from carrying out respiration. [2]

....

....

....

d. Respirometers B and D were set up as control experiments.

Describe the purpose of the controls in **this** investigation. [2]

....

....

Assignment support

You could use this technique to generate data for your Assignment.

You could investigate the effect of temperature on respiration in other organisms, for example blowfly larvae.

You could use a copy of the grid in **Appendix 4** to plan an Assignment based on this technique – use the checklist on pages v–vi to help.

6 Reaction time – Effect of practice on reaction time

Background biology

The nervous system carries nerve impulses along nerves very quickly. When a receptor detects a stimulus, sensory neurons carry impulses into the central nervous system (CNS) to be processed through inter neurons. The CNS sends impulses out through motor neurones to effectors such as muscles to bring about a response. The reaction time can be thought of as the time from the detection of the stimulus to the making of the response.

Learning outcomes

- Know and understand that the nervous system carries nerve impulses to and from the CNS.
- Process information by calculating averages.
- Present information as a bar chart.
- Evaluate experimental procedures and suggest improvements.

Aim

To investigate differences in individual human reaction times.

Apparatus list

- half-metre stick (1)
- lab stool (1)
- conversion table, distance to time (1; see **Appendix 1**)

Experimental precautions

- You should not allow practice before taking the reaction time tests.

Method

1. Have the subject sit on a stool with their hand out in front of them with their wrist resting on a bench as shown in the diagram.

2. **The subject should be aware that they must catch the half-metre stick as soon as they see it start to move**.

   Drop a half-metre stick as shown, without warning.

Figure 6.1

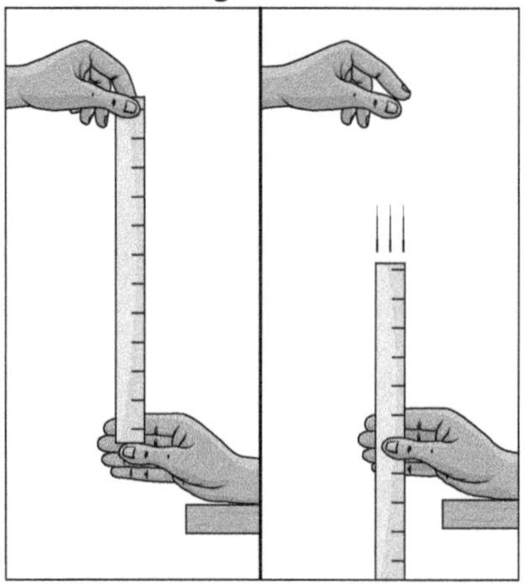

3. Record, in the table below, the distance that the metre stick has travelled before being caught.

4. Repeat the procedure 10 times.

5. Repeat steps 1–3 with a second subject.

6. Convert drop distances to reaction times using the values in **Appendix 1** and record them in the table below.

7. Calculate the average reaction time for each subject.

Record your results

Attempt	Distance fallen (cm) Subject 1	Reaction time (s) Subject 1	Distance fallen (cm) Subject 2	Reaction time (s) Subject 2
1				
2				
3				
4				
5				
6				
7				
8				
9				
10				
Averages				

Draw a bar chart to show the average reaction times for each subject.

Figure 6.2

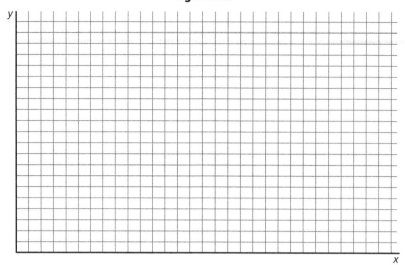

Check your understanding

1. Write **two** conclusions which can be made from the results of this experiment. [2]

....

....

....

2. Suggest a way in which the reliability of this experiment could be improved. [1]

....

....

Exam-style question

Some researchers investigated the changes to reaction time when individuals were given doses of a new drug. The individual volunteers were given different masses of the drug then asked to take a reaction time test in which they had to press a lever when a light flashed. The results are shown in the table below.

Mass of drug consumed (units)	Reaction time (milliseconds)
0	190
1	200
2	210
3	230
4	270
5	320
6	380

a. Write a conclusion which can be drawn regarding the effect of the drug on reaction time. [1]

....

....

b. Calculate the percentage increase in reaction time when 6 units of the drug are consumed compared with no drug. [1]

.... %

c. Calculate the ratio of reaction time after 1 unit of drug compared with after 5 units. [1]

       1 unit : 5 units

      .... : ....

d. Explain how the individual who was given none of the drug acted as a control in this experiment. [2]

....

....

e. Suggest how the reliability of this experiment could be improved. [1]

....

....

Assignment support

You could use this technique to generate data for your Assignment.

You could investigate the effect of age or gender on reaction time, or the effect of distractions such music playing or the effect of the presence of an audience.

You could use a copy of the grid in **Appendix 4** to plan an Assignment based on this technique – use the checklist on pages v–vi to help.

7 Potometer – Effect of surface area on transpiration rate from geranium leaves

Background biology

Transpiration is the process of water moving through the xylem of a plant and its evaporation through the stomata in the lower epidermis of leaves. Water vapour moves out of the leaf through stomata on the leaf surfaces. A potometer is a device which can be used to measure the volume of water a leaf takes up in a set period of time. We can assume that this water is eventually transpired.

Factors which affect transpiration rate include temperature, wind speed, humidity and the leaf surface area.

Learning outcomes

- Know and understand that plant leaves lose water to the air by transpiration.
- Process information by calculating averages.
- Process information by calculating leaf surface area.
- Present information as a line graph.
- Draw valid conclusions from experimental results.
- Evaluate experimental procedures and suggest improvements.

Aim

To measure the effect of leaf surface area on transpiration.

Apparatus list

- geranium or other potted plant with leaves (1)
- scissors (1 pair)
- micro **test tubes** or Bijou bottles (3)
- **measuring cylinder** (1×10 cm^3)
- **dropper** (1)
- paraffin or olive oil (few cm^3)
- marker pen and ruler (1)
- modelling clay or a micro test tube rack (1)
- squared paper (supply)
- safety glasses (pair each)

Experimental precautions

- Ensure that your leaf stalk is well below the water level before you add the surface oil.

Method

1. Set up three micro test tubes in a rack or support then with modelling clay as shown in the drawing on the next page.

2. Measure out 5 cm^3 of water and add it to each test tube. Mark the water level with a marker pen.

3. Select three leaves of different surface areas and draw round them onto a piece of squared paper. Later, estimate the surface area of each leaf by counting the squares covered – **remember to multiply your answer by 2 because there are two surfaces**.

4. Snip each leaf from the plant ensuring that you have a long stalk on each.

5.   Add each leaf to a separate micro test tube and carefully add a drop of oil onto the water surface in each tube.

Figure 7.1

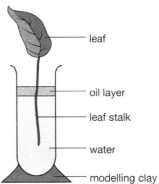

6.   Leave the potometer on a side bench overnight at least.

Record your results

1.   The next day, use a ruler to measure how much the water level has dropped in each tube.
     Complete the results table below.

Surface area of leaf (cm³)	Water loss (mm)

2.   Plot your results on the graph paper below. Remember to include scales, labels and units.

Figure 7.2

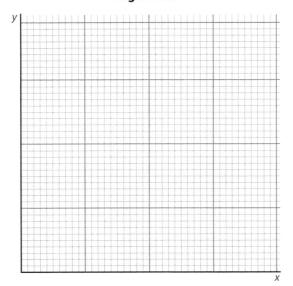

Check your understanding

1. Write a conclusion based on the aim of your experiment.   [1]

    ....

    ....

2. Make a list of **three** variables which were controlled in your experiment.   [3]

    1. ....

    2. ....

    3. ....

3. Suggest how the reliability of the results could be increased.   [1]

    ....

    ....

Exam-style question

The rate of transpiration in plants can be measured using the potometer shown below.

As the plant transpires, coloured water is drawn up the glass tube and its volume measured, over a set period of time, to give the rate of transpiration.

Figure 7.3

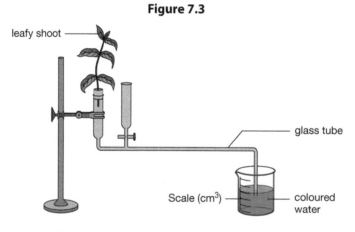

a. Changes in the surrounding environment can have an effect on the rate of transpiration.

    State the effects of the following environmental changes on the rate of transpiration.   [3]

    Increase in humidity ....

    Increase in temperature ....

    Increase in wind speed ....

b. Choose any of the environmental changes listed above.

    Describe an addition to the **apparatus shown** which would allow an investigation into
    its effect.   [1]

    ....

    ....

c. The graph below shows transpiration rates of two plants, X and Y.

Figure 7.4

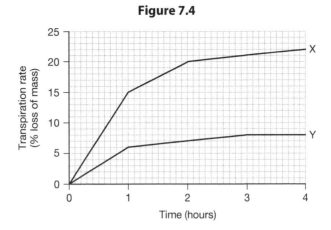

Suggest **three** possible reasons for the differences in transpiration rate between plants X and Y.   [3]

....

....

....

Assignment support

You could use this technique to generate data for your Assignment.

You could investigate the effects of humidity, wind speed or temperature on the rate of transpiration of one species or compare different species under the same conditions.

You could use a copy of the grid in **Appendix 4** to plan an Assignment based on this technique – use the checklist on pages v–vi to help.

8 Using a transect line – Measuring changes in the abiotic factors light intensity and soil moisture in a habitat

Background biology

The distribution of living organisms is affected by abiotic factors. These non-living factors include light intensity, moisture, pH and temperature. To measure the changes in these factors through a habitat, a transect line can be set up. A transect is a line passing through the habitat along which sampling stations can be set up.

Learning outcomes

- Know and understand that the distribution of organisms is affected by abiotic factors.
- Know and understand that a transect line can be used to locate sample stations through a habitat.
- Present information as a double-axis bar chart.
- Evaluate experimental procedures, identify sources of error and suggest improvements.

Aim

To investigate changes in the abiotic factors light intensity and soil moisture through a habitat.

Apparatus list

- 50 m measuring tape (transect line) (1)
- **light meter** (1)
- soil **moisture meter** with probe (1)
- paper towel (1)

Experimental precautions

- Ensure that your body does not shade the light meter when taking readings.
- Ensure that you wipe the moisture probe between readings.

Method

1. Lay out the 50 m transect line. Your teacher will discuss this with you.
2. At 5-metre intervals (stations) along the transect line, take:
   - a light meter reading
   - a soil moisture reading.

Record your results

1. Add your results to the table below.

Station	Light meter reading (units)	Moisture meter reading (units)
1		
2		

Station	Light meter reading (units)	Moisture meter reading (units)
3		
4		
5		
6		
7		
8		
9		
10		

2. Draw a double-axis bar chart of your results – put light meter reading on one *y*-axis and the moisture meter reading on the other. Draw two bars for each station – one for light intensity and the other for moisture.

Figure 8.1

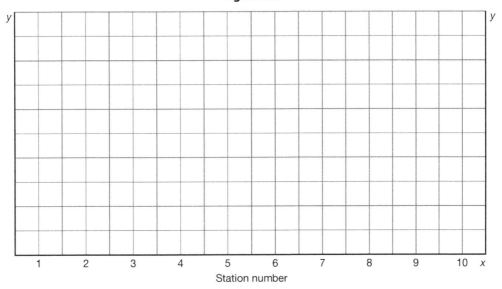

Station number

Check your understanding

1. Describe a source of error which could affect the results of each abiotic measurement.

   a. Light intensity reading [1]

   ....

   ....

   b. Soil moisture reading [1]

   ....

   ....

2. Suggest how abiotic factor measurements can be made more reliable. [1]

   ....

   ....

Exam-style question

In an investigation into the distribution of heather plants, six quadrats were dropped at stations along a transect line from the top to the bottom of a hill. Soil moisture, pH and surface light intensity were recorded at each station and heather abundance scores were recorded for each quadrat.

Figure 8.2

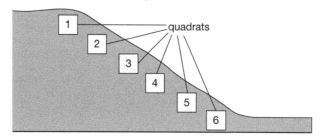

Station	Soil moisture (%)	Surface light intensity (lux)	pH	Heather abundance score
1	10	10 000	5·5	25
2	15	11 000	5·4	22
3	40	10 000	5·5	15
4	63	10 500	5·5	9
5	71	12 000	5·6	6
6	81	11 000	5·4	0

a. Describe the distribution of heather on the slope of the hill. [1]

....

....

b. Identify the abiotic factor which has the greatest effect on the distribution of the heather plants. [1]

....

c. Identify the quadrat that would be most likely to contain a species of plant which grows best in wet soil with a low pH. [1]

....

Assignment support

You could use this technique to generate data for your Assignment.

You could investigate how an abiotic factor affects the distribution of a common plant or invertebrate animal in or around your school grounds. This technique could be used along with those outlined in Experiment 9.

You could use a copy of the grid in **Appendix 4** to plan an Assignment based on this technique – use the checklist on pages v–vi to help.

9 Sampling with quadrats and pitfall traps – Measuring the distribution of daisy plants and invertebrates along a transect line

Method

1. Lay out the 50 m transect line where your teacher indicates. There will be a station every 5 metres to give 10 stations in all.

2. At stations 1, 5 and 10 set a pitfall trap as shown.

Figure 9.1

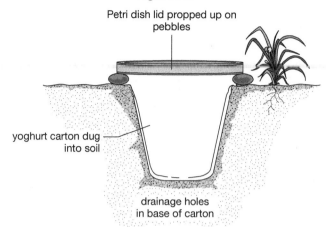

Petri dish lid propped up on pebbles

yoghurt carton dug into soil

drainage holes in base of carton

3. At each station drop a quadrat randomly, behind you over your shoulder.

4. Count the number of small squares which have the species you are interested in, for example daisy plants. Your teacher will make sure you know what the leaves look like as well as the flowers.

Record your results

1. Add your results to Table 1.

2. Present your quadrat results as a bar chart.

3. The next day, collect your pitfall traps. Empty the contents of each into a separate plastic tray. Use any keys you have to classify the invertebrates you find (see **Appendix 2**), count the numbers and record your results in Table 2.

   Make sure that you return the captured animals to the area where they were caught.

Table 1 Quadrat results

Station	Number of quadrat squares with daisy /25	Percentage of quadrat squares with daisy (%)
1		
2		
3		
4		
5		
6		
7		
8		
9		
10		

Bar chart of quadrat results

Figure 9.2

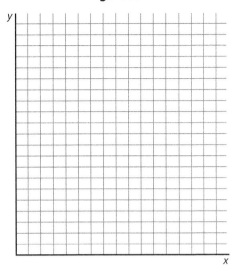

Table 2 Pitfall trap results

Invertebrate group	Numbers of each group of invertebrates		
	Station 1	Station 5	Station 10
Beetles			
Spiders/mites			
Centipedes			
Millipedes			
Slugs			
Snails			
Springtails			
Woodlice			
Worms			
Total			

Check your understanding

1. Suggest how sampling can be made more reliable. [1]

....

....

2. Describe any trend or pattern which can be seen in your quadrat samples [2]

....

....

3. Suggest why the following abiotic factors might affect the distribution of organisms. [3]

Light ....

Temperature ....

Soil water concentration ....

Exam-style question

During a woodland survey, a group of students measured some abiotic factors.

Readings they took included the temperature of the soil and the air.

a. Name **one** abiotic factor, other than temperature, which they could have measured in the woodland and describe the method of measuring this factor. [2]

....

....

b. During the survey, the students sampled the leaf litter in the woodland using pitfall traps. When they checked the pitfall traps four days after setting them up, the students discovered that they were all empty.

Describe **two** errors which could explain why there were no invertebrates in the traps. [2]

....

....

....

....

c. The errors were corrected and the students set out the pitfall traps once again.

The table below shows the types of invertebrates and numbers found.

Use the information in the table to complete the pie chart. [2]

Invertebrate group	Number found
Woodlice	35
Beetles	20
Slugs	0
Spiders	30
Snails	15

Figure 9.3

Assignment support

You could use this technique to generate data for your Assignment.

You could investigate the distribution of a common plant or invertebrate species in or around your school grounds.

You could use a copy of the grid in **Appendix 4** to plan an Assignment based on this technique – use the checklist on pages v–vi to help.

10 Measuring the rate of photosynthesis – Effect of light intensity on the rate of photosynthesis in *Cabomba*

Background biology

Photosynthesis is a enzyme-controlled process in which sugar is synthesised and oxygen is released. In photosynthesis light energy from the sun is trapped by chlorophyll in the chloroplasts. Light intensity is a limiting factor in photosynthesis. The rate of photosynthesis can be limited by the light intensity available. *Cabomba* plants take in CO_2 during photosynthesis and release it during respiration. Hydrogen carbonate indicator turns purple in a solution with a low CO_2 level and yellow if the CO_2 level is high. Plants which are photosynthesising at a high level compared with their respiration use up CO_2 quickly and turn indicator solutions purple. Plants which are respiring but not photosynthesising turn indicator solutions yellow.

Learning outcomes

- Know and understand that photosynthesis requires light and carbon dioxide.
- Present information as a bar chart.
- Draw valid conclusions from experimental results.
- Evaluate experimental procedures and suggest improvements.
- Make a prediction.

Aim

To show the effect of varied light intensity on photosynthesis.

Apparatus list

- Bijou bottles and caps (3)
- orange-red hydrogen carbonate indicator (30 cm³)*
- **funnel** or **syringe** (1)
- forceps (1 pair)
- *Cabomba* (supply; about 15 fronds needed)
- black paper (supply)
- thin white tissue paper (supply)
- clear tape (roll)
- fine marker pen (1)
- light bank (fluorescent tube) (in lab)
- sticky tape (1 roll)
- safety glasses (pair each)

Method

1. Use the forceps to add five fronds of *Cabomba* to each of the three empty Bijou bottles.
2. Use the funnel or syringe to fill the bottles of *Cabomba* equally with the orange-red hydrogen carbonate indicator.
3. Mark the lids with your initials then cap the bottles.
4. Wrap black paper around one of the bottles and tape down – this will represent zero light intensity.
5. Wrap a thin layer of white tissue around one of the bottles and tape down – this will represent dim light.
6. Place all three bottles in front of a fluorescent tube and leave for 40 minutes – the uncovered bottle represents bright light.

Record your results

1. Note any colour changes of the hydrogen carbonate indicator in the table below.

2. Use words from the key below to describe the rate of photosynthesis in each tube.

Light intensity	Colour of indicator at start	Colour of indicator after 40 minutes	Rate of photosynthesis
dark	orange-red		
dim	orange-red		
bright	orange-red		

Key
yellow	=	zero photosynthesis
orange-red	=	very low rate of photosynthesis
magenta	=	low rate of photosynthesis
purple	=	high rate of photosynthesis

3. Draw a bar chart of your results on the graph paper below.

Figure 10.1

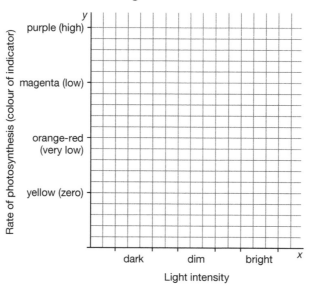

Check your understanding

1. Write a conclusion about the effect of light intensity on the rate of photosynthesis in *Cabomba*. [1]

   ....

   ....

2. Give **two** variables which have been controlled in this experiment and for each suggest an improvement to that control. [4]

   Variable 1 ....

   ....

   Variable 2 ....

   ....

Exam-style question

Some students set up apparatus as shown in the diagram. They set the lamp at different distances from the pond weed to vary the light intensity and at each distance they counted the oxygen bubbles produced in 1 minute. Their results are shown in the table.

Figure 10.2

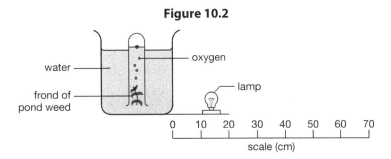

Distance between lamp and pond weed (cm)	Number of bubbles counted in 1 minute
10	45
20	46
30	44
40	30
50	21
60	12
70	5

a. Identify **one** variable which the students should control to make the results valid. [1]

....

b. Predict the number of bubbles which would be produced if the experiment were repeated with the lamp at 25 cm from the pond weed. [1]

....

....

c. Describe how increasing the light intensity affects the rate of photosynthesis in the pond weed. [2]

....

....

Assignment support

You could use this technique to generate data for your Assignment.

You could investigate various factors which might affect rates of photosynthesis, such as light intensity, colour of light, temperature and availability of CO_2.

You could use a copy of the grid in **Appendix 4** to plan an Assignment based on this technique – use the checklist on pages v–vi to help.

Distance (cm)	Reaction time (s)	Distance (cm)	Reaction time (s)	Distance (cm)	Reaction time (s)
1	0·05	34	0·26	67	0·37
2	0·06	35	0·27	68	0·37
3	0·08	36	0·27	69	0·38
4	0·09	37	0·27	70	0·38
5	0·10	38	0·28	71	0·38
6	0·11	39	0·28	72	0·38
7	0·12	40	0·29	73	0·39
8	0·13	41	0·29	74	0·39
9	0·14	42	0·29	75	0·39
10	0·14	43	0·30	76	0·39
11	0·15	44	0·30	77	0·40
12	0·16	45	0·30	78	0·40
13	0·16	46	0·31	79	0·40
14	0·17	47	0·31	80	0·40
15	0·17	48	0·31	81	0·41
16	0·18	49	0·32	82	0·41
17	0·19	50	0·32	83	0·41
18	0·19	51	0·32	84	0·41
19	0·20	52	0·33	85	0·42
20	0·20	53	0·33	86	0·42
21	0·21	54	0·33	87	0·42
22	0·21	55	0·34	88	0·42
23	0·22	56	0·34	89	0·43
24	0·22	57	0·34	90	0·43
25	0·23	58	0·34	91	0·43
26	0·23	59	0·35	92	0·43
27	0·23	60	0·35	93	0·44
28	0·24	61	0·35	94	0·44
29	0·24	62	0·36	95	0·44
30	0·25	63	0·36	96	0·44
31	0·25	64	0·36	97	0·44
32	0·26	65	0·36	98	0·45
33	0·26	66	0·37	99	0·45

This is only one example of a very simple paired statement key which could be used to find the basic group into which an invertebrate can be classified.

1.	Legs	go to 4
	No legs	go to 2
2.	Head with feelers	go to 3
	Head with no feelers	**worm**
3.	Shell	**snail**
	No shell	**slug**
4.	Three pairs of legs	go to 5
	More than three pairs of legs	go to 6
5.	Wing cases	**beetle**
	Small and jumping	**springtail**
6.	Four pairs of legs	**spider or mite**
	More than four pairs of legs	go to 7
7.	Seven pairs of legs	**woodlouse**
	More than 7 pairs of legs	go to 8
8.	Two pairs of legs per segment	**millipede**
	One pair of legs per segment	**centipede**

Appendix 3 Notes for teachers

Hydrogen carbonate indicator

1. **Stock solution**
   - Dissolve 0·10 g of cresol red and 0·20 g of thymol blue in 20 cm^3 of ethanol.
   - Dissolve 0·85 g of sodium hydrogen carbonate in about 200 cm^3 of freshly boiled (and cooled) distilled water.
   - Add the cresol red/thymol blue solution produced in step 1 to the hydrogen carbonate solution produced in step 2 and dilute with 1 litre of freshly boiled (and cooled) distilled water.
2. **Experimental solution**
   - Dilute the stock solution by a factor of 10 with freshly boiled distilled water and bubble air through this diluted solution to equilibrate it with atmospheric carbon dioxide.

Iodine solution

- Dissolve 6 g of potassium iodide in about 200 cm^3 of distilled water.
- Add 3 g of iodine crystals.
- Make the solution up to 1 litre with distilled water.

Starch agar plates (for five plates)

- Add 2 g of agar to 100 cm^3 of 0·2% starch solution.
- Autoclave and pour plates when cooled to 55°C, allowing 20 cm^3 per plate.

Appendix 4 Assignment planning grid

This grid is to be used for practice only.

Section	Description	Marks
Title		1
Aim		1
Underlying biology		3
Data collection and handling		6
Graphical presentation		4
Analysis		1
Conclusion		1
Evaluation		2
Structure	This mark will automatically be awarded if you have followed the above structure.	1
Total		**20**

Answers

1 Estimating plant cell size

Check your understanding

1. So that cells do not cover each other and are easier to observe [1]
2. To make the cells more easily visible/easier to count [1]
3. **a.** 5000 µm [1]
   b. 500 µm [1]
   c. 50 µm [1]

Exam-style question

a. **i.** Length = 300 µm [1]
   Height = 120 µm [1]
   ii. 5 : 2 [1]
b. 8 µm [1]
c. Measure the field of view (in micrometres) at ×100 [1]
   Make a stained cheek cell slide [1]
   Estimate how many cells can be seen across the field of view at ×100 [1]
   Divide the field diameter by the number of cells [1]

2 Osmosis

Check your understanding

1. The lower the water concentration, the more the tissue loses weight/water by osmosis [1]
2. Shape/surface area of potato tissue
   Same potato
   Volume of solution used
   Temperature
   Time in solutions [any 3, 1 each]
3. Repeat the experiment (and find average of mass changes) [1]

Exam-style question

a. −0·21 [1]
   −10% [1]
b. Starting masses of tissue not the same [1]
c. A solution which gave no change in mass would be equal in concentration to the tissue; 5% gives an increase and 10% gives a decrease so somewhere in between is equal. [2]

3 Measuring enzyme activity 1

Check your understanding

1. Different plant tissues have different concentrations/amounts of catalase [1]
2. Temperature
   Mass of tissue
   Time for reaction
   Volume/concentration of hydrogen peroxide [any 3, 1 each]
3. Masses of tissue slices could be different [1]
   Weigh to determine mass [1]
   OR
   Bubbles of oxygen foam might burst [1]
   Collect gas in a separate tube/use detergent to make the foam bubbles stronger
   Measure the volume of oxygen collected [1]

Exam-style question

a. Scales and labels with units [1]
   Accurate plots connected by straight lines [1]
b. As the temperature increased up to 40°C the rate of reaction increased [1]
   But as the temperature increased above 40°C the rate of reaction decreased [1]
c. Same set-up but change pH in each tube (using buffers/acid or alkali) [1]
   Keep temperature constant [1]

4 Measuring enzyme activity 2

Check your understanding

1. As temperature increases the activity of diastase increases then deceases [1]
2. Number of grains added to each dish
   Concentration of starch in agar
   Mass of agar in each dish
   Time left [any 3, 1 mark each]
3. Extent to which grains are pushed into the agar [1]
   Make a mash of grains and add to a well in the agar [1]

Exam-style question

a. Scale and labels including units [1]
   Accurate plots joined by straight lines [1]
b. As the pH increases from 5 to 7 the activity of diastase increases [1]
   But as pH rises further to pH 10 the activity of diastase decreases [1]
c. 3.0 mm [1]

5 Using a respirometer

Check your understanding

1. As temperature increases, the rate of respiration increases [1]
2. Mass/number of seeds
   Width of the respirometer arm
   Age of germinating peas as extra option
   Volume of air in tube at start
   Time for respiration [any 3, 1 each]
3. Temperature of the respirometer may physically affect the volume of gases within [1]
   Ensure enough time is allowed for gases to come to correct/experimental temperature before stopper is added [1]

Exam-style question

a. 1·3 mm per minute [1]
b. Increasing temperature increases the rate of respiration in pea seeds
   OR
   Dead peas do not respire [1]
c. High temperature denatures enzymes [1]
   Respiration is an enzyme-controlled process [1]
d. Control allows comparison with experiment [1]
   To show that it is the peas which use up the oxygen in the respirometer [1]

6 Reaction time

Check your understanding

1. Reaction time varies from person to person [1]
Practice in this technique improves measured reaction time [1]
2. Repeat the experiment more times with the same person/using more subjects [1]

Exam-style question

a. As the mass of drug consumed increases/the more drug taken the slower the reaction time [1]
b. 100% [1]
c. 5 : 8 [1]
d. To compare to the drug treatment to show that differences in reaction time were due to the drug [2]
e. Repeat the investigation with more individuals/ volunteers/subjects [1]

7 Potometer

Check your understanding

1. The larger the surface area, the greater the rate of water uptake/transpiration [1]
2. Temperature
Wind speed
Humidity
Initial volume of water supplied [any 3, 1 each]
3. Repeat the procedure using more and obtain an average [1]

Exam-style question

a. Increase in humidity – decrease in transpiration [1]
Increase in temperature – increase in transpiration [1]
Increase in wind speed – increase in transpiration [1]
b. Increase in humidity – place a plastic bag over the shoot and tie off [1]
Increase in temperature – place apparatus in a constant temperature chamber [1]
Increase in wind speed – place a fan/hair-dryer beside the apparatus [1]
c. X is in higher temperature
X has more stomata/higher surface area
X is in higher wind speed
X is in lower humidity OR converse for Y [any 3]

8 Using a transect line

Check your understanding

1. a. Shading light meter sensor with body [1]
   b. Failing to wipe probe between readings [1]
2. Repeating the measurements (and calculating averages) [1]

Exam-style question

a. The further down the slope the less heather plants are found/heather abundance decreases [1]
b. Soil moisture [1]
c. Quadrat 6 [1]

9 Sampling with quadrats and pitfall traps

Check your understanding

1. Increase the number of samples taken [1]
2. Description of trends or patterns in results [2]
3. Light – can affect rate of photosynthesis [1]
Temperature – can affect rate of enzyme-controlled reactions [1]
Soil water concentration – can affect osmosis/turgidity [1]

Exam-style question

a. Light intensity [1]
Use a light meter [1]
OR
pH
Use a pH meter
Soil moisture [1]
OR
Use a soil moisture meter [1]
b. Left out too long and predated within trap [1]
Rim of trap above soil surface [1]
c. Correct sizes of segments [1]
Correct labels on segments [1]
Woodlice = 7
Beetles = 4
Slugs = 0
Spiders = 6
Snails = 3

10 Measuring the rate of photosynthesis

Check your understanding

1. Light is required for photosynthesis/as the light intensity increases the rate of photosynthesis increases [1]
2. Number of *Cabomba* fronds [1]
Weigh instead of count [1]
Fill both bottles with indicator [1]
Measure equal volumes of indicator [1]

Exam-style question

a. Temperature
OR
Time left to photosynthesise [1]
b. 45 bubbles [1]
c. As light intensity increases the rate of photosynthesis increases [1]
As light intensity increases further the rate of photosynthesis remains steady [1]